An old story retold
by Friedel Steinmann (drawings)
and Dieter Kohl (text)

WILLIAM B. EERDMANS PUBLISHING COMPANY
GRAND RAPIDS, MICHIGAN

This old story tells us
~~how the world~~
was destroyed in a great flood.
It shows us what caused this flood
and why nonetheless not everything
came to an end.

Strictly speaking this is
the story not of a catastrophe
but of a rescue.

3

The Bible does not tell much about the people who lived at that time. In one place it merely says, "They paid no heed to anything."

Not that they were exceptionally bad . . .

. . . but God no longer had a place in their lives, except for:

O my God, what a hot day again . . .

Thank God we have a shady spot here . . .

or . . .

. . . and bless this young couple . . .

or . . .

. . . and comfort those who are left behind mourning . . .

. . . and . . .

. . . dear God, please let me not get a C in penmanship tomorrow . . .

But to God that was not enough.

The story begins on a mild spring evening in a small town.

7

In this town lived a man named Noah.

He sat in his room reading awhile before going to bed.

Suddenly . . .

NOAH!

10

Noah was given exact instructions for the ship.

11

12

13

Already the following morning Noah started his difficult task.

14

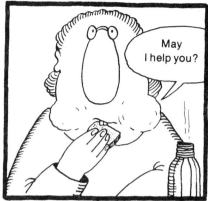

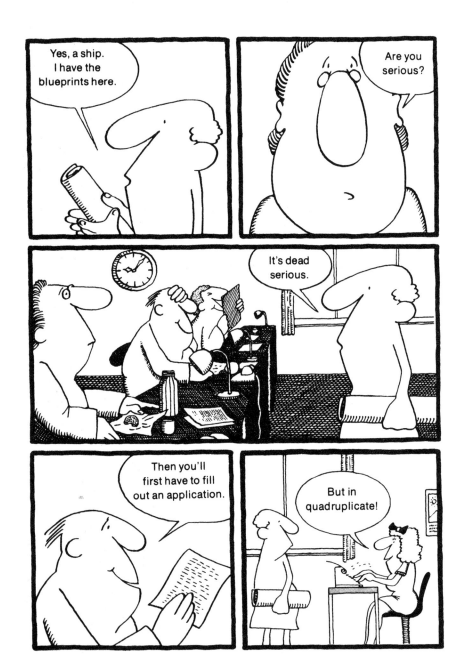

19

20

21

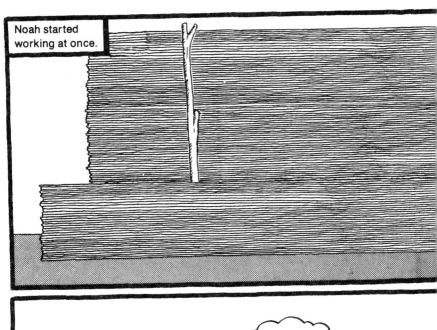

23

24

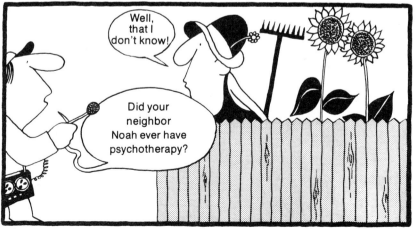

25

Soon the whole city knew about it.

EVENING PO

26

28

29

33

From near and far
the people came
to admire the attraction.

34

There was something for everyone.

Smile a little more, please!

Boat pendants were in great demand.

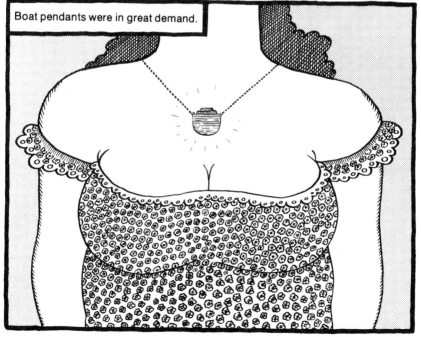

35

One liked it this way . . .

. . . the other that way . . .

I like it with waves around it.

Boat tattooing

Almost everyone agreed: The ship was a smash hit.

♪ You are my . . . When skies a

BEER ON TAP

1 Beer $1
1 Popcorn

Even lovebirds found things to do.

The people went back
to their regular work again.
Still, once in a while
they wondered a bit.

41

42

Except for a few children who happened to be playing nearby . . .

. . . nobody paid attention, because they had other things to worry about.

Hope we get some relief soon.

43

44

45

46

48

49

56

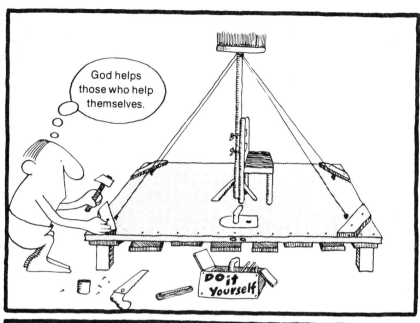

59

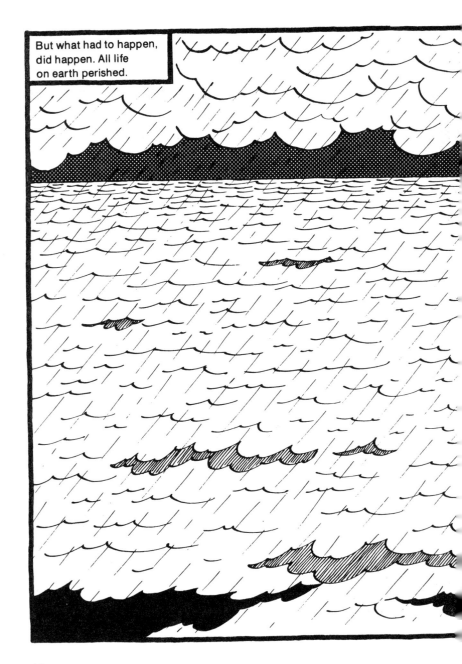

But what had to happen, did happen. All life on earth perished.

Ex-
ception

The floods went down. Man had been given a new opportunity. Has he made use of it? We read of God that He again had to provide salvation.

For God so loved the world that he gave his only Son, that whoever (whoever!) believes in him should not perish but have eternal life.